THOMAS CRANE PUBLIC LIBRARY
QUINCY MA

CITY APPROPRIATION

Louisiana

Rich Smith

Visit us at
www.abdopublishing.com

Published by ABDO Publishing Company, 8000 West 78th Street, Suite 310, Edina, Minnesota 55439 USA. Copyright ©2010 by Abdo Consulting Group, Inc. International copyrights reserved in all countries. No part of this book may be reproduced in any form without written permission from the publisher. The Checkerboard Library™ is a trademark and logo of ABDO Publishing Company.

Printed in the United States.

Editor: John Hamilton
Graphic Design: Sue Hamilton
Cover Illustration: Neil Klinepier
Cover Photo: iStock Photo

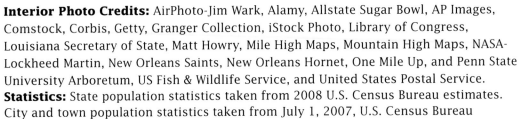

Manufactured with paper containing at least 10% post-consumer waste

Interior Photo Credits: AirPhoto-Jim Wark, Alamy, Allstate Sugar Bowl, AP Images, Comstock, Corbis, Getty, Granger Collection, iStock Photo, Library of Congress, Louisiana Secretary of State, Matt Howry, Mile High Maps, Mountain High Maps, NASA-Lockheed Martin, New Orleans Saints, New Orleans Hornet, One Mile Up, and Penn State University Arboretum, US Fish & Wildlife Service, and United States Postal Service.

Statistics: State population statistics taken from 2008 U.S. Census Bureau estimates. City and town population statistics taken from July 1, 2007, U.S. Census Bureau estimates. Land and water area statistics taken from 2000 Census, U.S. Census Bureau.

Library of Congress Cataloging-in-Publication Data

Smith, Rich, 1954-
  Louisiana / Rich Smith.
     p. cm. -- (The United States)
  Includes index.
  ISBN 978-1-60453-653-9
  1. Louisiana--Juvenile literature. I. Title.

  F369.3.S64 2010
  976.3--dc22
                          2008051044

Table of Contents

The Pelican State

Louisiana is an important center of American trade, commerce, and ideas. The mighty Mississippi River reaches the Gulf of Mexico by flowing through the state. This makes Louisiana a gateway to the rest of the world. More goods come and go from ports in Louisiana than in any other state in the United States.

Another reason for Louisiana's importance is its people. They come from many lands and speak many languages.

Few places are better to live, work, and play in than Louisiana. It has beautiful beaches in the south, glorious uplands in the north, and magnificent cities in between. It is known as the Pelican State because of the great number of brown pelicans found along its coastline.

Louisiana is known
as the Pelican State.

Quick Facts

Name: Louisiana was named in honor of Louis XIV, who was king of France from 1643-1715.

State Capital: Baton Rouge, population 227,071

Date of Statehood: April 30, 1812 (18th state)

Population: 4,410,796 (25th-most populous state)

Area (Total Land and Water): 51,840 square miles (134,265 sq km), 31st-largest state

Largest City: New Orleans, population 239,124

Nicknames: Pelican State, Bayou State, Sugar State

Motto: Union, Justice and Confidence

State Bird: Brown Pelican

State Flower: Magnolia

State Tree: Bald Cypress

State Song: "Give Me Louisiana" and "You Are My Sunshine"

Highest Point: Driskill Mountain, 535 feet (163 m)

Lowest Point: New Orleans, -8 feet (-2 m)

Average July Temperature: 82°F (28°C)

Record High Temperature: 114°F (46°C), August 10, 1936, in Plain Dealing

Average January Temperature: 52°F (11°C)

Record Low Temperature: -16°F (-27°C), February 13, 1899, in Minden

Average Annual Precipitation: 64 inches (163 cm)

Number of U.S. Senators: 2

Number of U.S. Representatives: 7

U.S. Postal Service Abbreviation: LA

Geography

Louisiana is located along the coast of the Gulf of Mexico in the southern United States. Its neighbor to the north is Arkansas. To the west is Texas. South is the Gulf of Mexico. The Mississippi River forms most of the state's eastern border. On the other side of it is the state of Mississippi.

Louisiana is the 31st-largest state. It covers 51,840 square miles (134,265 sq km).

All of Louisiana belongs to the Gulf Coastal Plain region of the southern United States. That means the land surface of Louisiana is mostly flat and low. It is the third-lowest place in the nation. The lowest point within Louisiana is the city of New Orleans. It is 8 feet (2 m) below sea level.

ARKANSAS

Shreveport

LOUISIANA

TEXAS

Sabine River

Mississippi River

MISSISSIPPI

Baton Rouge

Lake Charles   Lafayette

Lake Pontchartrain

New Orleans

N

0   100 miles
0   100 km

GULF OF MEXICO

Louisiana's total land and water area is 51,840 square miles (134,265 sq km). It is the 31st-largest state. The state capital is Baton Rouge.

The highest point in Louisiana is Driskill Mountain in the north. However, it is not very high at all. It is only 535 feet (163 m) above sea level.

Driskill Mountain is located in a part of Louisiana known as the Uplands region. Cutting through these wooded uplands are long, narrow stretches of alluvial plains. In the middle of these plains are major rivers.

The most important rivers in Louisiana are the Mississippi, Red, Pearl, Atchafalaya, Vermilion, Teche, Calcasieu, Boeff, Mermentau, Lafourche, and Sabine. The largest inland body of water in Louisiana is Lake Pontchartrain on the edge of New Orleans.

Along the coast of Louisiana are nearly 2,500 small islands. The southeastern portion of the Louisiana coast is known as the Coastal-Delta section. Swamps, marshes, and bayous are found in great numbers along the entire south coast from Texas to Mississippi.

Louisiana is filled with rivers, lakes, swamps, marshes, and bayous.

Climate and Weather

Summers in Louisiana are very hot and humid. The average July temperature is close to 82°F (28°C). Winters are mild. The average January temperature is nearly 52°F (11°C).

The reason for these temperatures is that Louisiana has a subtropical climate. That means it is similar to the climate found at the earth's equator.

Louisiana receives a lot of rainfall during the year because of its subtropical climate. Average rainfall is about 64 inches (163 cm).

Hurricanes sometimes strike Louisiana and cause great damage. One of the worst hurricanes ever to hit the state was named Katrina. It had been growing stronger for days in the warm waters of the Gulf of Mexico before reaching land on August 29, 2005.

About 1,500 people in Louisiana were killed by this storm. Many drowned when the levees that kept New Orleans dry collapsed from the battering wind, rain, and high tides. New Orleans is below sea level, so nothing could stop the water from flooding in once the protection of the levees was gone.

The strong winds of Hurricane Katrina pound two men as they fight their way to find shelter in August 2005.

Plants and Animals

The bald cypress is the most famous tree in Louisiana. It is a graceful tree with leaves that look like feathers. The leaves fall off in winter, and that is how the word "bald" got into the tree's name. The water-loving bald cypress is often found in swamps and bayous. It grows 80 to 130 feet (24 to 40 m) tall and between 7 to 10 feet (2 to 3 m) in diameter.

Other trees that grow in Louisiana include shortleaf pine, slash pine, longleaf pine, tupelo, beech, eastern red cedar, and black walnut.

The state's official flower is the magnolia. It grows from the branches of the magnolia tree. The tree grows 65 to 100 feet (20 to 30 m) tall. The flower blossoms in the late spring and has a pleasing smell.

Spanish moss hangs from cypress trees in Louisiana's Atchafalaya National Wildlife Refuge.

Louisiana Iris

Found mainly in and near marshes is the Louisiana iris. This beautiful bloom is the state's official wildflower.

Louisiana is home to many types of animals. The black bear is the state's official mammal. Black bears grow to 6 feet (2 m) in length and weigh 400 pounds (181 kg) or more. They are very smart. They eat just about anything, but like berries and nuts most of all.

Other animals of Louisiana include bobcats, deer, opossums, minks, raccoons, skunks, rabbits, bats, mice, and snakes. The American alligator is the state's official reptile. The green tree frog is its official amphibian. The honeybee is the official insect.

The brown pelican is the official bird of Louisiana. The state also has turkeys, quails, ducks, bald eagles, hawks, owls, egrets, blue herons, and many more birds.

Swimming in Louisiana's waters are catfish, bass, gar, and more. The white perch is the state's official fish.

An alligator family in a Louisiana swamp.

Black Bears

Blue Heron with Catfish

Bobcat

History

It was many thousands of years ago that the first people arrived in what is now Louisiana. These Native American tribes formed the Choctaw and Natchez Nations, among others.

Hernando de Soto

Hernando de Soto of Spain was one of the first Europeans to travel through Louisiana. He visited in 1541, searching for gold. He never found any. That is one reason why Spain wasn't very interested in colonizing Louisiana.

An explorer from France by the name of René-Robert Cavelier de La Salle claimed Louisiana and all neighboring lands for his own country in 1682. He named Louisiana Territory in honor of King Louis XIV.

The first permanent French settlement was Fort St. Jean Baptiste at the present-day city of Natchitoches. It was founded in about 1716. Two years later, the city of New Orleans was founded. New Orleans became the capital of France's entire Louisiana Territory in 1723.

René-Robert Cavelier de La Salle claimed Louisiana for France in 1682.

An event was held in New Orleans on December 20, 1803, celebrating the Louisiana Purchase.

France went to war with Great Britain in 1754 and lost. But before losing, France gave Spain most of Louisiana Territory rather than let Great Britain take it. Spain gave Louisiana Territory back to France in 1800. Three years later, France sold it to the young United States. Louisiana Territory was later split into 15 new states. Louisiana was one of them. It was admitted to the Union on April 30, 1812. That made Louisiana the 18th state.

Louisiana quickly became famous for growing cotton and sugar cane. It took so many people to raise and harvest these crops that farmers started using slaves from Africa as helpers. Because of the slaves' hard work, the cotton and sugar cane farms grew bigger and bigger. These vast farms were known as plantations.

Sugar cane farms grew into successful plantations with the help of many slave workers.

The plantations depended so much on slavery that Louisiana refused to free slaves when the United States

The Battle of Baton Rouge occurred on August 5, 1862, when Confederate troops tried to recapture their capital city. Union troops held the city.

federal government demanded it. This refusal led to the American Civil War. Louisiana and 10 other Southern states wanted to keep slavery legal. They decided to start their own country. Beginning in 1861, Confederate troops fought bloody battles against the Northern states' Union soldiers for four years. In 1865, Louisiana and the rest of the Confederacy were defeated. The United States was reunited. Slaves were freed.

The economy of Louisiana was a mess for a long time after the Civil War. Things did not really begin to improve until 1928. That year a governor by the name of Huey Long was elected.

Governor Long ordered the building of modern bridges, highways, schools, hospitals and more. These construction projects put many thousands of people to work during the darkest days of America's Great Depression. Long's efforts helped Louisiana become the mighty state it is today.

Huey Long was Louisiana's governor from 1928 to 1932.

Did You Know?

- Louisiana's southern and central regions are known as Cajun Country. This began in the 1750s when many French colonists from Canada's Nova Scotia province fled to Louisiana to avoid a war. Nova Scotia at the time was called Acadia. The people from the area were called Acadians. In French, Acadian is pronounced *Ah-cah-jan*. Their new neighbors in Louisiana soon began calling them Cajuns for short, and the name stuck. Today, many ancestors of these Acadians live in Louisiana. Their rich culture is celebrated around the state.

- It's a crime to bite someone in Louisiana. But it's a worse crime if you bite someone and you're wearing false teeth.

- A golden spike was frequently used as the final spike in the last piece of track laid on a new railroad. The first woman to have the honor of pounding down a golden spike was Julia Rule of Louisiana. It happened on July 12, 1884, during ceremonies to mark completion of a railroad serving the city of Shreveport.

- Louisiana has the tallest state capitol building in the United States. It is 34 stories tall.

People

Terry Bradshaw (1948-) was a quarterback who led the Pittsburgh Steelers to four Super Bowl championship titles in six years. He began playing professional football in 1970 and retired in 1983. He was inducted into the Pro Football Hall of Fame in 1989. He became a sports announcer and went into acting after his football career ended. Bradshaw was the first National Football League player to receive a star on the Walk of Fame in Hollywood, California. He was born in Shreveport, Louisiana.

Bryant Gumbel (1948-) is a well-known television sportscaster and news personality. He was a co-host of the popular NBC morning program *The Today Show* from 1982 to 1997. Since then, he has hosted the HBO series *Real Sports with Bryant Gumbel.* He served as a play-by-play announcer of National Football League games for two seasons, beginning in 2006. Gumbel has won four Emmy Awards and numerous other honors during his television career. He was born in New Orleans.

Author **George Washington Cable** (1844-1925) wrote against the mistreatment of African Americans in the time following the Civil War. His novels captured the hard life of many Louisiana Creoles. Cable was a friend of famous writer Mark Twain. The two authors often teamed up to speak to groups of people. Cable was born in New Orleans.

Ferdinand "Jelly Roll" Morton (1885-1941) was a piano player, composer, and bandleader. He is remembered as one of Louisiana's cool jazz creators. The recordings he and his band made in the 1920s are true classics. Morton was born in New Orleans.

Edward Douglass White (1845-1921) was the ninth person to serve as chief justice of the United States Supreme Court. He held the position from 1910 until his death in 1921. White joined the Supreme Court in 1894. Before that, he was a United States senator. White is said to have served in the Confederate army during the Civil War. That would make him the only Supreme Court justice ever to have waged war against the United States. He was born in Thibodaux, Louisiana.

Cities

New Orleans was founded in 1718. The city is famous for its yearly Mardi Gras

New Orleans is known as "The Big Easy."

celebration. It's also known for great food, jazz music, interesting buildings, and Creole culture. New Orleans is sometimes called "The Big Easy" for the easy-going spirit of its people. Normally, New Orleans is the largest city in Louisiana. In 2000, the population was 484,674. In 2006, it had dropped to 210,198. Where did everyone go? People left because of the terrible flooding and damage caused in 2005 by Hurricane Katrina. Recovery is slow, but New Orleans is being cleaned up and rebuilt. Today, its population is 239,124.

Baton Rouge is the capital of Louisiana. It is Louisiana's second-largest city, with a population of 227,071. After Hurricane Katrina damaged New Orleans in 2005, many people moved temporarily to Baton Rouge. As New Orleans continues rebuilding, people are returning to their homes there. Baton Rouge is a major transportation center. It also hosts a thriving industry that makes plastic and other products. Baton Rouge is located about 75 miles (121 km) up the Mississippi River from New Orleans. The city's nickname is "The Red Stick," which is what its French name means in English.

Baton Rouge is the capital of Louisiana.

The population of **Shreveport** is 199,569. That makes it the third-largest city in the state. Shreveport was founded in about 1836. It is located on the Red River in the northwest corner of Louisiana. It is sometimes called "The Port City" or "The River City." Tourism, gambling, retail, and services are very important to Shreveport's economy.

The fourth-largest city in Louisiana is **Lafayette**. Its population is 113,544. The city was founded in 1821. Lafayette's south-central Louisiana location is the reason the city calls itself the "Heart of Cajun Country." But Cajun is not the only culture celebrated in Lafayette. The city also honors the culture of the Creoles.

Lake Charles is the state's fifth-biggest city. Its population is 70,270. Lake Charles is another important place for Cajun culture. The city's nickname is the "Festival Capital of Louisiana." More than 100 pageants and carnivals are held there each year.

Transportation

The Port of South Louisiana is one of the busiest sea and river ports in the Western world. The port is 54 miles (87 km) long and stretches along both banks of the

The Port of New Orleans sees ships and freighters of all sizes travel up the Mississippi River carrying millions of tons of cargo.

Mississippi River between the ports of New Orleans and Baton Rouge.

Great international ships and freighters can travel up the Mississippi River only as far as the Port of Baton Rouge. Smaller cargo ships and barges travel on. Almost two-thirds of all the grain grown in the United States passes through Louisiana's ports.

Cargo unloaded from ships visiting these ports leaves the docks by train and by truck. Louisiana has many miles of track and highway for these vehicles.

A much smaller amount of freight is transported by air. There are about 200 airfields in Louisiana. The state also has more than a dozen bases for seaplanes.

Lakefront Airport was built in 1934 on a man-made peninsula that juts into Lake Pontchartrain. It has since been expanded. Today, it is used by commercial, private, and military aircraft.

Natural Resources

Louisiana's 26,800 farms cover nearly 8 million acres (3 million hectares) of land. That is more than 25 percent of the total land area of the state. Many products are grown. Cotton, rice, beef, and soybeans are four of the most important. Louisiana is also the nation's second-biggest producer of sugar cane.

Fish farms are common in Louisiana. Crawfish and catfish are raised on fish farms. But Louisiana's biggest hauls of fish come from the waters of the Gulf of Mexico.

Crawfish, oysters, shrimp, and crabs are on display in a New Orleans market.

Louisiana's commercial fishing industry is among the largest in the nation. Most prized among the catches are shrimp, oysters, and menhaden.

Oil drilling rigs are set up across the state of Louisiana, as well as offshore in the Gulf of Mexico.

Almost half of Louisiana is forest. From these timberlands come more than 1 billion board feet (2.4 million cubic meters) of lumber each year.

The mines of Louisiana produce salt, industrial sand and gravel, and lignite. Also

Lignite is also called brown coal.

from the earth beneath Louisiana comes crude oil and natural gas.

Industry

Louisiana is an important state for refining oil and producing oil-based products. The state has 19 working oil refineries. Only

The Mississippi River runs past an oil refinery near Garyville, Louisiana.

Texas has more refining capacity. The nation's single largest refinery is in Louisiana. So is the last refinery to be built in the United States.

Aerospace is another important Louisiana industry. The Michoud Assembly Facility near New Orleans builds parts for NASA's newest spaceships. The vehicles are designed to transport people to Mars and beyond.

NASA chose Michoud for this work because Louisiana is home to a growing number of

Workers at the Michoud Assembly Facility in New Orleans walk beside a space shuttle external tank.

companies that make super-strong, super-lightweight, advanced materials.

Louisiana companies not only build spaceships, but also water-going vessels. More than 25 percent of the cargo ships built in the United States come from Louisiana shipyards.

Other important industries in Louisiana are tourism, entertainment, shipping, information technology, and medical research.

Sports

Louisiana has two major league and two minor league sports teams. The New Orleans Saints are part of the National Football League. The New Orleans Hornets are part of the National Basketball Association. The Bossier-Shreveport BattleWings are a minor league Arena Football team. The Louisiana Swashbucklers from Lake Charles are part of the Indoor Football League.

One minor league and two independent baseball clubs play in Louisiana. They are the New Orleans Zephyrs, the Shreveport-Bossier Captains, and the Alexandria Aces. Minor league hockey is played by the Bossier-Shreveport Mudbugs.

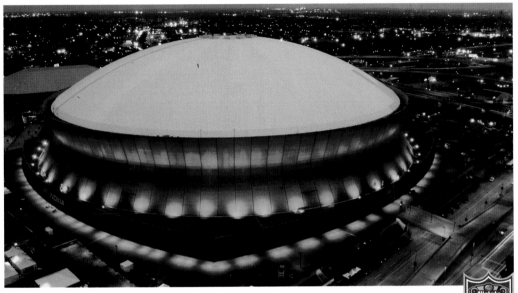
The Sugar Bowl is played in New Orleans's Superdome.

College sports are big in Louisiana. One of the biggest college events is the annual Sugar Bowl. It is the second-oldest bowl game in the United States. It is held around New Year's Day each year in New Orleans.

Louisiana has 20 state parks and many historic and recreation sites. People enjoy everything from fishing and swimming to hiking and camping.

Entertainment

New Orleans is famous for its jazz clubs and music.

Louisiana is one of the most entertaining places in America. It is very difficult to be bored living or visiting there.

The center of entertainment in Louisiana is New Orleans. The city has many famous jazz clubs and places where live shows are performed. Some of the best of these are found along Bourbon Street in the city's historic French Quarter.

Huge crowds flock to New Orleans each winter to attend Mardi Gras. This gigantic celebration features a number of colorful parades and fun parties. People get into the spirit of the event by dressing up in strange costumes.

Mardi Gras
is one of
hundreds
of major
festivals
held in

Thousands of people
come to New Orleans every year for Mardi Gras.

Louisiana throughout the year. There is a festival for just about everything having to do with the state's history, wildlife, ethnic groups, music, art, food, and traditional crafts.

In addition to festivals, Louisiana also has a number of great museums, historical monuments, orchestras, theaters, and libraries.

Timeline

5000 BC—First humans arrive in Louisiana. They later group into various Native American tribes.

1541—Spanish explorer Hernando de Soto travels through Louisiana.

HERNANDO DE SOTO

1682—France claims a vast slice of America and names it Louisiana.

1716—Fort St. Jean Baptiste becomes the first permanent settlement within the future state of Louisiana. It is built by the French near the present-day city of Natchitoches.

1718—The city of New Orleans is founded.

1803—France sells Louisiana Territory to the United States.

1812—Louisiana becomes the 18th state.

1861—Louisiana and 10 other Southern states break away from the United States in order to keep slavery legal. This causes the start of the American Civil War.

1865—The Confederacy is defeated. Slaves are freed and the Civil War ends.

1901—Oil is discovered in Louisiana.

1928—Huey Long is elected governor. He begins modernizing the state.

2005—Hurricane Katrina destroys much of New Orleans. Rebuilding begins at once.

Glossary

Alluvial Plains—Low, flat areas where clay, dirt, gravel, and sand have been deposited by previously fast-moving rivers and streams.

Bayou—A lowland stream, river, or lake that flows very slowly.

Civil War—The war fought between America's Northern and Southern states from 1861-1865. The Southern states were for slavery. They wanted to start their own country. Northern states fought against slavery and a division of the country.

Confederacy—Louisiana and 10 other Southern states that broke away from the United States. This caused the American Civil War, which lasted from 1861 until 1865.

Creole—People whose ethnic heritage is a mix of French and Spanish; or French, Spanish and African; or French, Spanish, African, and Native American.

Great Depression—Beginning in 1929, a time when many businesses failed and millions of people lost their jobs.

Hurricane—A violent wind storm that begins in tropical ocean waters. Hurricanes cause dangerously high tides and bring deadly waves, driving rain, and even tornadoes. Hurricanes break up and die down after reaching land.

Levee—An earthen or concrete wall that protects low ground from being flooded by a nearby body of water.

Mardi Gras—A festival to celebrate the arrival of Lent. Lent is the 40 days before Easter. Many Christians observe this time by not eating for one or more days. Mardi Gras takes place the day before Lent begins on what is called Ash Wednesday. Mardi Gras is an occasion to eat lots of food. The name Mardi Gras in French means "Fat Tuesday."

National Aeronautics and Space Administration (NASA)—A U.S. government agency started in 1958. NASA's goals include space exploration, as well as increasing people's understanding of Earth, our solar system, and the universe.

Index

NQ